For Paula and Stephen
MB
For Eva, Iván, Olov, and Naná
JV

First US edition 2024
First published by Nosy Crow Ltd. (UK) 2023

Library of Congress Catalog Card Number pending
ISBN 978-1-5362-3427-5

APS 29 28 27 26 25 24
10 9 8 7 6 5 4 3 2 1

Printed in Humen, Dongguan, China

This book was typeset in Berylium.
The illustrations were created digitally.

Candlewick Press
99 Dover Street
Somerville, Massachusetts 02144

www.candlewick.com

MOIRA BUTTERFIELD   **ILLUSTRATED BY JESÚS VERONA**

LOOK
WHAT I FOUND
on the Farm

Today we're on the farm. Let's go!
Through the gate where daisies grow.

Look what I found!

A tuft of sheep's wool, as soft as my
favorite sweater.

FARM
WALK

Can you also find . . .
- One scarecrow?
- Two blue butterflies?
- Three white sheep?

A farm is a place for growing crops or raising animals. Farmers usually live close to the fields where their animals graze and their crops grow.

A sheep has a thick, woolly coat called a fleece. Sometimes, if a sheep brushes past a fence, it can leave tiny tufts of its fleece behind. Once a year, a sheep's thick fleece is shorn, or shaved off, and it might be made into wool for knitting.

A farm can be home to all kinds of animals. Look for sheep with black or white faces, shaggy coats, or long, curly horns.

Cows can be black, brown, cream, or white—or sometimes splotched with colors. There are different breeds of cow, such as Holstein, Jersey, or Highland.

ANIMAL FOOTPRINTS TO FIND:

Cow

Two fat, curved shapes, like giant beans

Sheep

Two long shapes, like bunny ears

Horse

A curved, upside-down "U" shape from the horse's metal shoe

Chicken

Three pointy lines that connect at one end

Who's that in the pen?
Cheeping chicks with mother hen.

Look what I found!
A family of goats!

Can you also find . . .
- One white hen?
- Two munching goats?
- Three eggs that haven't hatched yet?

Most animals are born in springtime,
when the weather is warmer and there's
plenty of food for them to eat.

When a chick is ready to hatch, it will peck its way out of the
shell using a sharp point on the end of its beak called an egg
tooth. It takes an entire day and night. No wonder chicks
need a rest once they hatch!

When chicks first hatch, they look damp and straggly. But they soon
dry out and become fluffy.

Ducks hatch in springtime, too. The ducklings will follow their mom in a line to the pond, to swim and find food together.

Newborn lambs are very wobbly on their legs, so they are not able to stand up right away. Their mother licks them clean as they practice getting to their feet.

ANIMAL BABIES TO FIND:

Chick

Chicks can be yellow, brown, white, or black.

Lamb

Lambs form strong connections with their mothers.

Calf

Calves need to feed on their moms' milk to grow.

Duckling

Ducklings have little pointy wings and big feet.

Foal

Foals stay close to their mothers when they're first born.

Grass is growing, green and sweet—
just right for a horse to eat.

Look what I found!
A grass stalk I can put between
my thumbs and blow. Squeeeeak!

Can you also find ...

- One tractor?
- Two swooping birds?
- Three horses?

In springtime, the grass starts growing in the field. This is the perfect food for horses, cows, and sheep.

In late spring, the grass needs to be cut. The cuttings will be dried out in the sun and made into bales of hay for the animals to eat when winter comes again.

The hay is stored in a barn to keep it dry. If the hay gets damp, it will get moldy and the animals won't be able to eat it.

Farm animals are usually kept in barns through the winter, but as soon as it's warm enough they are let out into grass fields. It can be exciting to be outside, and they can be seen wandering around the fields.

Grasses with soft tufts of flowers

Feathery, fluffy grasses that wave in the breeze

Droopy grasses that bend over in an arch shape

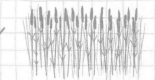

Long, spiky grasses that stand up straight

Along the path there's lots to see,
which means a game for you and me.

Look what I found!
Fluffy balls of dandelion seeds.
Blow on one and make a wish.

Can you also find . . .
- One mouse hiding?
- Two spiderwebs?
- Three ladybugs?

Hedges are leafy homes for plants and animals.
They give shelter from the wind and rain.

Small birds and little animals make nests in
the leafy shadows of a hedge or bush, away from
bigger animals that might want to eat them. It's a
safe home for insects, too.

Blowing on a ball of dandelion seeds is a popular
way to make a wish. What do you wish for?

The dandelion seeds will float away in the wind and new dandelions will grow where the seeds land.

Wildflowers often grow under the shelter of a bush or hedge. It's OK to pick dandelions, but it's important not to pick the other flowers you might find so that they can grow.

TYPES OF INSECTS TO FIND:

Bumblebee
It collects pollen from flowers.

Butterfly
It drinks the sweet flower nectar.

Spider
It spins its webs between the branches.

Beetle
It munches on plants or hunts other insects.

Aphid
It feeds on leaf juice called sap.

Birds are perching in the trees.
Their songs float over on the breeze.

Look what I found!
A broken and empty eggshell,
blue as the sky and dotted with
freckles.

Can you also find . . .
- One squirrel?
- Two rabbits?
- Three blackbirds?

Wild birds build their nests in bushes and trees, and even in the barns on the farm. When baby birds hatch, their broken eggs sometimes fall to the ground.

Some animals build their homes on the ground—or even underground. Wild rabbits live in a burrow of underground tunnels called a warren. They pop up to nibble the grass.

Bigger wild animals such as foxes or badgers might live in quiet corners of a field. A fox's underground home is called a den, and a badger's home is called a sett.

ANIMAL HOMES TO FIND:

Large entrance hole

Foxes or badgers might live here.

Medium entrance hole

Rabbits might live here. Their droppings could be scattered around the entrances.

Small entrance hole

Rats or mice might live here.

Nest

The bigger the bird, the bigger the nest they build.

Blossom petals drifting down,
like confetti to the ground.

Look what I found!
An apple blossom petal,
soft as velvet between my fingers.

Can you also find . . .
* One watering can?
* Two bird feeders?
* Three birds?

Life on the farm changes throughout the year as different crops and fruits grow. Some farms have a stand where you can buy fresh food that has been grown.

The fruit trees blossom in spring and grow fruit in the summer. Delicious apples, pears, and strawberries will be ready to pick by mid- to late summer.

The bees that live on the farm make honey during the spring and summer. In winter, they rest in their hives.

In summer, crops such as wheat and barley grow taller and taller in the fields, ready to be harvested before winter comes. Wheat will be turned into flour— perfect for bread and cakes.

Milk from cows, goats, or sheep on the farm can be turned into other foods such as butter, cheese, yogurt, or ice cream.

CROPS AND FRUIT TO FIND:

Wheat

Wheat stalks grow in spiky tufts called ears.

Oats

Grains of oat are made into oatmeal and oat bars.

Barley

Grains of barley are used to make all sorts of things, including breakfast cereal.

Fruit

Look for fruit such as mini crab apples and apricots.

We've seen the farm and walked around.

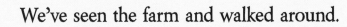

Look at all the things we've found . . .

TREASURE!

As you collect, be thoughtful, too.
Bring no harm with what you do.

When you're exploring the farm, always have an adult with you
and be careful around farm animals and wild animals.
Remember that it's their home, so always pick up after yourself
and don't leave any garbage behind.